SCHOLASTIC
News
Nonfiction Readers®

This Is the Way We Go to School

By Laine Falk

Children's Press®
An Imprint of Scholastic Inc.
New York Toronto London Auckland Sydney
Mexico City New Delhi Hong Kong
Danbury, Connecticut

These content vocabulary word builders are for grades 1–2.

Subject Consultant: Eli J. Lesser, MA, Director of Education, National Constitution Center, Philadelphia, Pennsylvania

Reading Consultant: Cecilia Minden-Cupp, PhD, Early Literacy Consultant and Author, Chapel Hill, North Carolina

Photographs © 2010: Alamy Images: 11, 21 center left, 23 top (William Casey), 5 top left (Corbis UK-Fancy), 2, 4, 22 center (David R. Frazier Photolibrary, Inc.), 13 top, 20 right center (Imagestate Media Partners Limited-Impact Photos), 6, 23 bottom (John Kershaw), 5 top right (Chris Rout), 9, 20 center left (Doug Steley A), 7, 20 center right (VisualJapan); Bryan and Cherry Alexander Photography: 15, 20 right; Corbis Images: cover (Tibor Bognar), 19 top, 21 left center (Bryn Colton/Assignments Photographers); Getty Images/Stuart Fox: 1, 19 bottom, 21 left; iStockphoto/Eric Isselée: 16, 22 bottom; John Warburton-Lee Photography/Nigel Pavitt: 17 top, 20 left center; PhotoEdit/Richard Hutchings: 5 bottom left, 21 center right; Reuters/Nasser Nuri: 13 bottom, 21 right, 22 top; Superstock, Inc./Francisco Cruz: 5 bottom right, 20 left; Victor Engelbert: back cover, 17 bottom, 21 right center.
Map 20-21: Jim McMahon

Art Direction and Production: Scholastic Classroom Magazines

Library of Congress Cataloging-in-Publication Data

Falk, Laine, 1974-
This is the way we go to school / Laine Falk.
      p. cm. – (Scholastic news nonfiction readers)
Includes bibliographical references and index.
ISBN 13: 978-0-531-21341-4 (lib. bdg.) 978-0-531-21440-4 (pbk.)
ISBN 10: 0-531-21341-2 (lib. bdg.) 0-531-21440-0 (pbk.)
1. Schools–Juvenile literature. 2. School children–Transportation–Juvenile literature.
I. Title. II. Series.
LB1556F35 2009   371.7–dc22   2009010908

CONTENTS

How Do You Go to School?

Do you take a **bus** to school? Do you ride in a car? Kids around the world go to school in many ways. Let's see how they get there!

bus

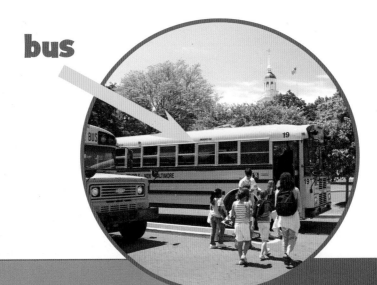

These children go to school in the United States.

On Tracks and Wheels

Some children in big cities may take a **subway** to school. A subway is a train that runs underground.

subway

These children take the subway to school in Japan.

A **bicycle** can be a fast and fun way to get to school. Children in many places ride their bikes.

This girl lives in a big city. She rides by tall buildings on her way to school. She always wears a helmet!

This girl rides her bicycle to school in Australia.

bicycle

9

Would you like to ride to school like these children?

They are in a **pedicab**. A pedicab has a big seat with wheels. A man pedals to make it go. The pedicab moves like a bicycle.

pedicab

These children take a pedicab
to school in Vietnam.

Over Water and Snow

Some children live near the water. They may take a **boat** to school.

Kids have to hold up their backpacks when they ride in a boat. They don't want their homework to get wet!

These children take a boat to school in Peru.

boat

These children take a boat to school in Egypt.

Other children live where snow falls all winter. Their mom or dad may drop them off in a **snowmobile**.

A snowmobile drives on top of deep snow. These children almost never miss school because of snow!

GUTTALUK SCHOOL
ᔅ ᐃᓄᐃᑦ

These children ride a snowmobile to school in Canada.

snowmobile

On Animals and On Foot

Would you like to ride a **donkey** to school? Would you rather ride a **horse**?

Some children live far from school. Riding animals gets them there in time.

donkey

These children ride donkeys to school in Sudan.

These children ride horses to school in Ecuador.

horse

Children who do not live too far from school can walk there. No matter where they live, kids chat and have fun as they walk.

How do *you* get to school each day?

These children walk to school in England.

These children walk to school in South Africa.

19

Canada | United States | United States | Ecuador | Peru | England

KIDS AROUND THE WORLD

Look at this map. Can you match the children in the photos to the countries where they live?

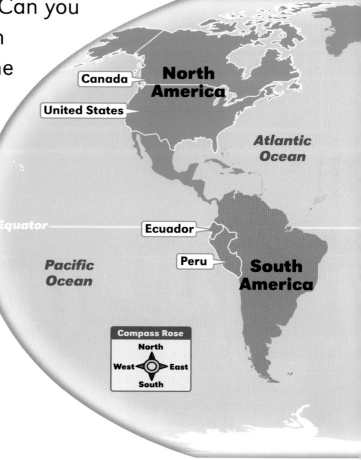

Egypt | South Africa | Sudan | Australia | Japan | Vietnam

GO TO SCHOOL

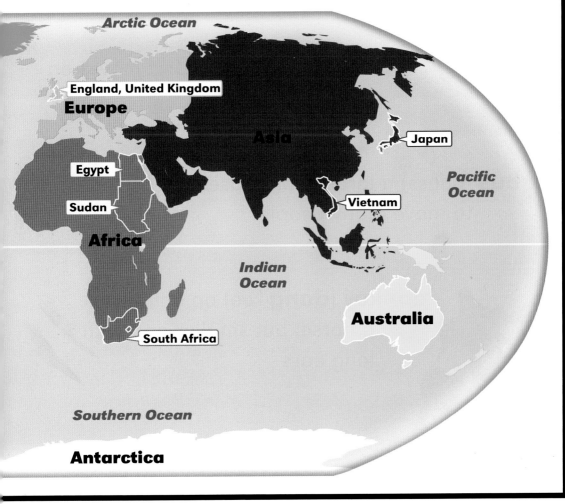

Arctic Ocean

England, United Kingdom

Europe

Asia

Japan

Egypt

Pacific Ocean

Sudan

Vietnam

Africa

Indian Ocean

South Africa

Australia

Southern Ocean

Antarctica

YOUR NEW WORDS

bicycle (**bye**-si-kuhl) a two-wheeled vehicle that you ride by moving the pedals

boat (bote) a vehicle that moves on the water

bus (buhss) a large vehicle used to move many people

donkey (**dong**-kee) an animal like a horse, but smaller and with long ears

horse (horss) a large, strong animal that people ride or use to pull things

pedicab (**ped**-ih-kab) a three-wheeled vehicle in which one person pedals and other people ride in a seat

snowmobile (**snoh**-moh-beel) a vehicle with an engine that moves over snow

subway (**suhb**-way) a system of trains that run underground in a city

INDEX

FIND OUT MORE
Book:
Morris, Ann. *On The Go*. New York: HarperCollins, 1994.

Website:
International Walk to School
http://www.iwalktoschool.org/photos/index.htm

MEET THE AUTHOR
Laine Falk is a writer and Scholastic editor. She lives in New York.
She used to take a school bus to school.